THE KIDS' BOOK OF AWESOME RIDDLES

Buster Books

Illustrated by
Andrew Pinder

Compiled by Amanda Learmonth
Edited by Katy Lennon
Designed by Jack Clucas
Cover design by John Bigwood

First published in Great Britain in 2019 by Buster Books,
an imprint of Michael O'Mara Books Limited,
9 Lion Yard, Tremadoc Road, London SW4 7NQ

 www.mombooks.com/buster
Buster Books
@BusterBooks

A CIP catalogue record for this book is available from the British Library.

ISBN: 978-1-78055-635-2

2 4 6 8 10 9 7 5 3 1

Papers used by Buster Books are natural, recyclable products made
from wood grown in sustainable forests. The manufacturing processes
conform to the environmental regulations of the country of origin.

Printed and bound in September 2019 by CPI Group (UK) Ltd,
108 Beddington Lane, Croydon, CR0 4YY, United Kingdom

FSC
www.fsc.org

MIX
Paper from
responsible sources
FSC® C020471

Introduction

Welcome to *The Kids' Book of Awesome Riddles*, a one-stop conundrum shop for budding riddlers. Challenge yourself with this cunning collection of riddles, brainteasers and conundrums, and when you have worked them out yourself, why not use them to puzzle your friends and family, too?

Just as exercise is good for the body, regular puzzling gives your brain a workout and can keep your mind super sharp. There's also the added feel-good factor of successfully solving a riddle using your brainpower alone.

All the answers are in the back of the book, so if you really struggle, take a peek. Reading the answer for one riddle could help you get your brain in gear and work out the next tricky brain-tickler.

Get ready to use some serious brainpower, solve the riddles and become a puzzle pro.

1. A squirrel, a bird and a monkey are racing to the top of a coconut tree. Who will reach the banana first?

2. Cows drink it and people have it in their coffee. What is it?

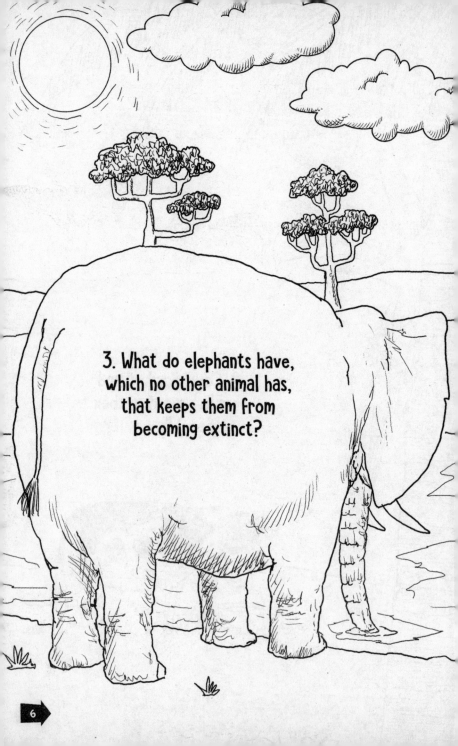

3. What do elephants have, which no other animal has, that keeps them from becoming extinct?

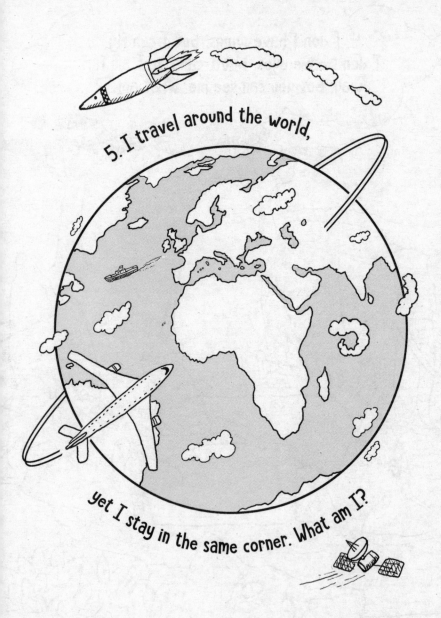

5. I travel around the world, yet I stay in the same corner. What am I?

8. You are alone in a dark room and have one match. There are also three objects: a candle, an oil lamp and a stove. What do you light first?

9. Three friends each have a different pet:
a cat, a parrot and a dog.

Gemma's pet can't fly.

Arthur's pet doesn't have fur.

Mohammed's pet doesn't bark.

Who has the pet cat?

10. There are ten chefs that all chop onions at the same speed. If it takes one chef 5 seconds to chop one onion, how long will it take ten chefs to chop ten onions?

11. I have fingers and a thumb but no flesh or bones. What am I?

12. Oliver's mother wakes him up for school. She asks him a question, but is sure from his answer that he is lying. What question did she ask to be so sure?

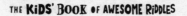

13. What lives in winter, dies in summer and grows upside down?

14. There are a few stones, a carrot and a scarf lying on the lawn. Nobody put them there. How did they get there?

15. Mahmut the bus driver did not sleep a single day for 2 months. How did he manage to do his job properly?

16. Down at the duck pond, a group of ducklings are paddling behind their mother. There are two ducklings in front of the duckling in the middle and three ducklings behind the two ducklings at the front. How many ducklings are there?

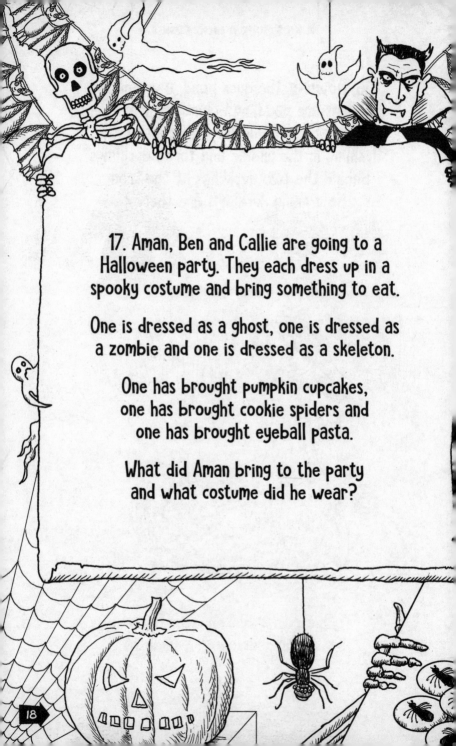

17. Aman, Ben and Callie are going to a Halloween party. They each dress up in a spooky costume and bring something to eat.

One is dressed as a ghost, one is dressed as a zombie and one is dressed as a skeleton.

One has brought pumpkin cupcakes, one has brought cookie spiders and one has brought eyeball pasta.

What did Aman bring to the party and what costume did he wear?

Here are some clues:

Ben brought the cookie spiders.

The person who brought the pumpkin cupcakes also dressed as a ghost.

Callie either brought the eyeball pasta or dressed as a skeleton.

18. A woman fell from a 100-step staircase, then walked away without a single bruise. How is this possible?

19. I hang in the sky, as birds pass me by,
but I'm always connected to the ground.

I dance in the breeze and I soar
up high without making a sound.

What am I?

20. George is painting a picture of a tree. He is just about to start adding the leaves, but he has run out of green paint. He checks his paint palette and sees that he only has blue, black, pink and yellow paint left. What does he do?

21. A tractor is on an island in the middle of a lake. There is no bridge that connects the island to the mainland. The tractor wasn't built on the island and it wasn't brought to the island on a plane or a boat. How did the tractor get there?

22. What moves under the sun but never casts a shadow?

23. A mother and her three children live in a pretty, round house. One day, the mother returns from work to find that the cookie jar is completely empty. She asks who ate all the cookies. The first child says he was busy doing his homework. The second child says she was out playing. The third child says he was reading in the corner. The mother didn't eat the cookies, so who did?

24. How many fingers do you have?

25. What can you hold in your left hand but can never hold in your right hand?

26. You are running in a race and you overtake the person who is in second place. What position are you in now?

27. I am as light as a feather, but even the strongest athlete in the world can't hold me for more than a few minutes. What am I?

28. Mr Simpson was killed on Tuesday afternoon. The police inspector came to investigate. Mr Simpson's wife told the inspector she was reading in her room at the time of the murder. The butler said he was having a bath. The chef said he was making breakfast. The gardener said she was planting flowers in the garden. Who killed Mr Simpson?

29. The more you take, the more you leave behind. What are they?

30. Dougal the dog is waiting for his owner outside a grocery store. He is attached to a 2-metre-long lead. Suddenly, a child's ball bounces into the street, 4 metres away. Dougal immediately dashes after it and returns the ball to the child. How is he able to do this?

31. What has two heads, one tail and walks on four legs?

32. What type of transport has eight wheels but can only carry one passenger?

33. Sally the postwoman is driving down the street in her van to deliver a package. She passes three doors: one pink, one green and one red. She can't remember which is the correct address, so she stops the van to have a think. Which door should she open first?

34. I have a kilo of gold
and a kilo of feathers.
Which weighs more?

35. If a rooster laid eight eggs and the farmer took four of them, and then another rooster laid six eggs but two of them cracked, how many eggs were left?

36. Mila washes her hair on Sundays and Wednesdays. If the day before yesterday was 2 days after the day before Wednesday, when is she next due to wash her hair?

37. Tom says he has a magic ball. He can throw
it as hard as possible and the ball will stop,
change direction and come back to him. He can
do this without the ball touching or bouncing
off anything. It is not tied to any string
or magnets. Is the ball really magic?

38. Romeo and Juliet have gone missing.
Inside their house there is broken
glass on the floor and a puddle of water
next to the dining table. The only other
living thing in the house is the pet cat.

Can you explain their disappearance?

39. Mrs McDonald, a maths teacher, decided to set her class the challenge of guessing her age. She told her class that in 4 years she will be twice as old as she was 20 years ago. How old is she?

40. All your cousins have the same uncle, but he isn't your uncle. How is this so?

World's
Best
Uncle

41. Two people left their house and went to the hospital. Three days later, three people left the hospital and returned to the same house. How can this be?

42. When is it bad luck for a black cat to cross your path?

43. A black cat crept out into the middle of a road. There were no street lights and it was cloudy. A car with its headlights switched off swerved around the cat. How did the driver know the cat was there?

44. I only come out at night.

I hang upside down to give you a fright.

If you come too close, you might get a bite!

What am I?

45. I'm tall when I'm young and short
when I'm old. I light up a pumpkin
on a Halloween night. What am I?

46. I can build castles, but I'm not made of bricks.
You can hold thousands of pieces of me in your hand.
What am I?

47. Why can't a man living in
France be buried in Spain?

48. Five brothers and sisters have come home from school.

Diego is playing on the computer.

Mateo is preparing a snack.

Sofia is playing table tennis.

Isabella is doing her homework.

What is the fifth sibling doing?

49. It's breaktime and the teacher has 20 oranges, but there are 23 children. How does she divide the oranges fairly between them?

50. Andrei has a fruit stall at the market. He sells apples not grapes, oranges not pineapples and cherries not raspberries. By the same logic, does he sell pears or strawberries?

51. When you don't need me, you ignore me. But whenever you make a mistake, you run to me for help. What am I?

53. Three farm workers were out working the fields in the rain. No one had a hat, hood or umbrella, but only two of them got their hair wet. How is this possible?

54. If you counted ten trees on your right going to school and ten trees on your left coming home, how many trees did you see in total?

55. An empty school bus pulls up to a stop and six children get on. At the next stop, three children get on, but one child, who has forgotten her homework, gets off. At the third stop, eight children get off. How many children are left on the bus?

56. Clara is having a lovely time playing on the beach.
She makes six little piles of sand in one place and
four bigger piles of sand in another place.
Then she decides to put them all together.
How many piles of sand does she have now?

57. On Orchard Street, the house numbers are set out in the following sequence: 1, 2, 3, 5, 8, 13. What is the next house number?

58. A footballer tried to score a goal 12 times. All but six times, the ball missed the net. How many goals did he score?

59. Danny and his friend are on their way to a football match to cheer on their favourite team. Danny says to his friend, "I know what the score will be before the game even starts!" His prediction turns out to be correct. What was it, and how did he know?

60. Sophie has four brothers and five sisters, but there are ten siblings. How is this so?

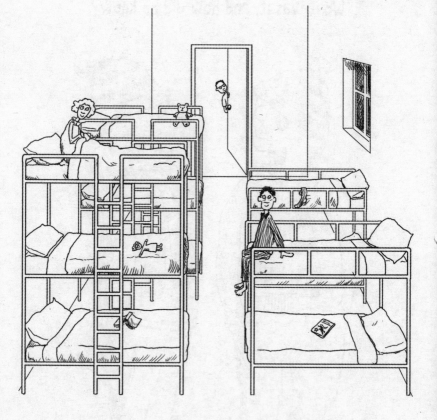

61. What belongs to you but your family and friends use it more than you?

62. Stella's mother has five daughters: Mimi, Momo, Mami and Memi. What is the fifth daughter's name?

63. Emilia is in a panic. She has left the bath running and it has flooded the bathroom. There is water all over the floor and it's starting to drip through to the floor below! She knows where the towels are kept, there's a mop in the cupboard downstairs and she has her phone at the ready to call her parents. What should she do first?

64. A woman has five daughters and they each have a brother. How many children does she have?

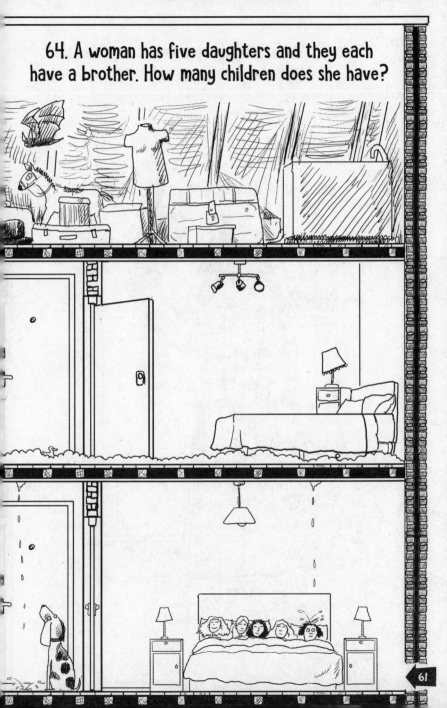

65. Why do you get less sleep in February?

66. If you multiply me by any other number, the answer will always be the same. What am I?

67. How many times can you subtract 10 from 100?

68. You want to boil an egg for 7 minutes but you only have a 2-minute hourglass timer and a 3-minute hourglass timer. How can you boil the egg for exactly 7 minutes?

69. You are my brother, but I am not your brother. Who am I?

70. There are five oranges and you take away four. How many do you have?

71. Summer is here, so I'm wearing green.
Autumn arrives, so it's time for a change.
Winter comes, so I get rid of my clothes.
What am I?

72. You're driving a bus from the city to the airport. The bus is travelling at an average speed of 80 kilometres an hour and makes six stops to pick up 20 passengers. By the time the bus arrives at the airport, it has 45 passengers on board and has travelled 60 kilometres. What is the bus driver's name?

73. You are trapped inside
a haunted house. It's very dark and
the lights don't work because there's no
electricity. You're feeling a bit nervous to
say the least! Suddenly, you hear a ghostly voice.
It tells you that in order to escape, you must
walk through one of three doors in front of you:

Behind door 1 is a room full of zombies.

Door 2 is wired with 10,000 volts,
which will fry you if you touch it.

Behind door 3 is a bottomless pit.

Which door do you choose?

74. Julio bought a bag of sweets on Monday.
He ate a quarter of them that day and
a third of them on Tuesday. On Wednesday
he ate half of the remaining sweets.
On Thursday there were two left.
How many were there to start with?

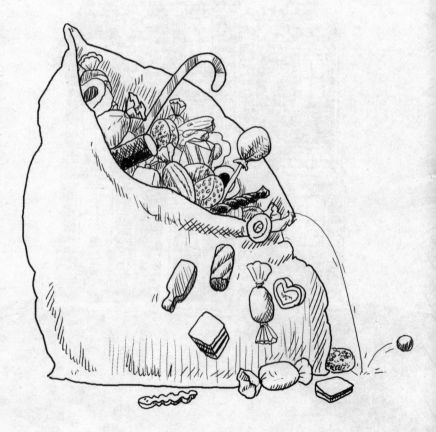

75. You use me to express your thoughts or jog your memory. If you drop me from the highest building, I won't break. But if you drop me into water, I won't survive. What am I?

76. Carlo lives on the 20th floor of a block of flats. Going to school every day, he takes the lift going down. But when he comes home, he takes the lift up to the 5th floor, then takes the stairs. Why does he do this?

77. Two friends, Martha and Oscar, make a bet as they each eat a bag of crisps. "I bet I can write your exact weight on a piece of paper," Martha says to Oscar. If Martha gets it wrong, she will give Oscar the rest of her crisps. If she gets it right, Oscar will give her the rest of his crisps. Martha has no access to any scales and has never weighed her friend before. In the end, Oscar has to give Martha his crisps. How did Martha win the bet?

78. A woman moves to a new town. She needs to get a haircut, so she goes in search of a hair salon. She notices that there are only two hair salons in town: the North End and the South End salons. Peering inside each one, she sees that the North End salon's hairdresser is well dressed and has a hairdo that's the height of fashion. The South End salon's hairdresser looks scruffy and old-fashioned. Which hair salon does the woman choose?

79. A criminal was sentenced to death for a crime she committed. The king granted her one last request: that she could choose how she died. The criminal made her choice and she was set free. How did this happen?

80. Three hikers, Naomi, Ana and David, want to cross a river. They find a boat with a sign saying 'Maximum weight 100 kg'. Naomi and Ana both weigh 50 kg, while David weighs 80 kg. How can they all cross the river using the boat?

81. Little Jenni is a rather fussy eater. She likes oranges not apples, eggs not cheese, avocados not cucumbers and bananas not grapes. Following the same rule, will she like melon or strawberries?

82. John goes into a pet shop to buy a parrot. He sees one with a sign on its cage that reads: 'I repeat everything I hear.' This sounds good to John, so he buys the parrot and takes it home with him. For three weeks he speaks to the parrot, but it doesn't say a word back. Disappointed, John takes the parrot back to the pet shop. But the shop owner says he was telling the truth about the parrot. How is this so?

83. You are locked in a room. The only way out is through one of two doors. One door leads to a cage made of magnified glass. If you stand in the cage even for a second, you will be frazzled by the blazing hot sun. Through the other door, you will find an enormous, fire-breathing dragon. How can you escape?

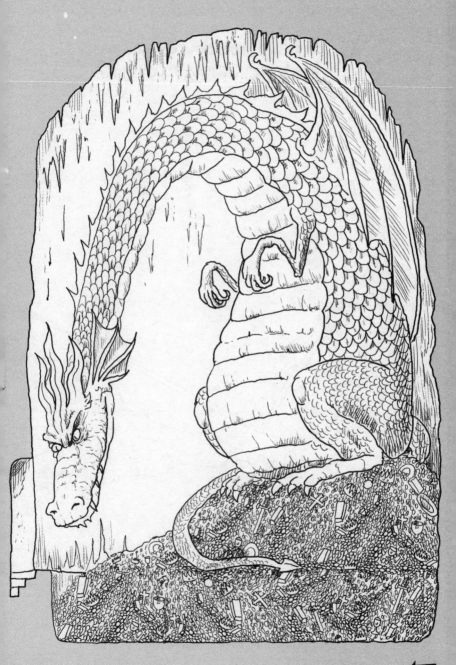

84. You draw a line. How can you make the line longer without touching it?

85. Three numbers give the same result when they are added together and multiplied together. What numbers are they?

86. Rosa and Toby take part in a race. Toby finishes first, yet Rosa is awarded the trophy for first place. She did not cheat or break any rules. Why did she win?

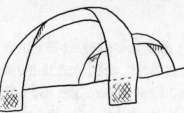

87. Kaya's mum sends Kaya on a shopping trip to buy some food for a dinner party. Kaya's mum instructs her NOT to buy anything red, as it will clash with her party colour scheme. Kaya returns with a pot of jam, some apples and some peppers. But Kaya's mum isn't angry. Why is this?

88. Imagine you are locked in a dark dungeon. All the doors are locked, the windows are barred and, even if you did manage to escape, you are surrounded by a moat full of man-eating crocodiles. What do you do?

89. Two fathers and their two sons go fishing along the river together. They each catch one fish to take home with them. They do not lose any fish on their way back. However, when they arrive at home they only have three fish between them. How can this be?

90. In a swimming race, Sandeep finished two places in front of Freddie, who came last. Sandeep finished one ahead of Isaac, who placed fourth. How many swimmers took part in the race?

91. Ten children are sitting in a circle, playing pass the parcel. They are all facing each other. A pesky fly is buzzing around them. Eventually it lands somewhere that everyone can see except for one child. Where does it land?

92. I can move up and down.
I can make you shiver
or make you sweat.
What am I?

93. A patch of daisies doubles in size every day. In 16 days it covers the whole lawn. How many days did it take to cover half the lawn?

94. If you ask this question every day of every month of every year, you'll never hear the same reply.
What is the question?

95. Four friends, Harry, Petra, Ramesh and Olivia, took part in a race. Harry didn't finish in first place and Petra didn't finish last. Ramesh was behind Olivia but ahead of Petra. How did they all place?

97. It never stops moving, but it has no legs. It cannot see, but it can be watched. Too much can cause boredom, too little can cause panic. What is it?

98. I cannot speak, but I will always talk back when spoken to. What am I?

99. The more you take from me the bigger I get. What am I?

100. At the sound of me, you may stamp your feet, laugh, sing or weep. What am I?

101. A girl goes into a store with just 50p. She buys a device that can add, multiply and subtract, write in any language and delete any mistakes. It is so small it can fit in her pocket. It doesn't run on batteries or electricity. What is it?

Olá

x

Bonjour

喂

hyvää päivää

Σ

∞

$-$

$\sqrt{}$

Shwmae

$\times$

$\int$

$+$

Hola

Hello

$\div$

$=$

God dag

π

$\%$

Bongu

102. Three friends, Maia, Sam and Anika, go to a café. On today's menu is:

A slice of cake

A strawberry milkshake

A cucumber sandwich

A ham roll

They each choose one different item from the menu.

Maia orders something sweet.

Anika is a vegetarian.

Sam is allergic to milk and bread.

Who orders the cucumber sandwich?

103. What do you see once in tennis, twice in table tennis, but never in golf?

104. A man is sitting in his cabin in Canada. Two hours later, he gets out of his cabin and finds himself in New York. How is this possible?

105. What has eight legs and flies?

106. Some people believe in me and some people don't.

Sometimes I rattle and sometimes I float.

What am I?

107. Creeping on my
belly, silent as the night,

Eyes forever open,
beware my nasty bite.

What am I?

108. What will you find in Norway and Finland but not in Sweden?

109. An old king feared that his children weren't clever enough to spend his fortune wisely. When the king died, he instructed that the key to the royal safe be placed inside one of three envelopes. The other two envelopes would be empty.

If the children could work out which envelope contained the key, they would inherit their father's fortune. But if they guessed incorrectly, they would get nothing. The children were not allowed to touch the envelopes. Their decision had to be made based on the statements written on the envelopes. The children were told that only one envelope had a true statement written on it and that the other two statements were false.

The following statements were written on the envelopes:

Envelope 1: This envelope does not have the key

Envelope 2: This envelope has the key

Envelope 3: The second envelope does not have the key

Which envelope should the children pick?

110. What can you take away the whole from, but some will still remain?

111. What type of lion never roars?

112. What do these letters all have in common?

A Y T M H W

113. A bus driver is heading towards the train station. He passes a stop sign without stopping, he turns right where there is a 'no right turn' sign and he goes down a one-way street in the wrong direction. There are two policemen nearby, but they don't take any notice. Why is this?

114. What stays hot even when kept in the fridge?

115. My feet stay warm, but my head is cold.

No one can move me, I'm just too old.

What am I?

116. What word is always spelled wrong in every dictionary?

117. A king, a queen and two twins lie still in a large room, yet there are no adults or children present. How is this possible?

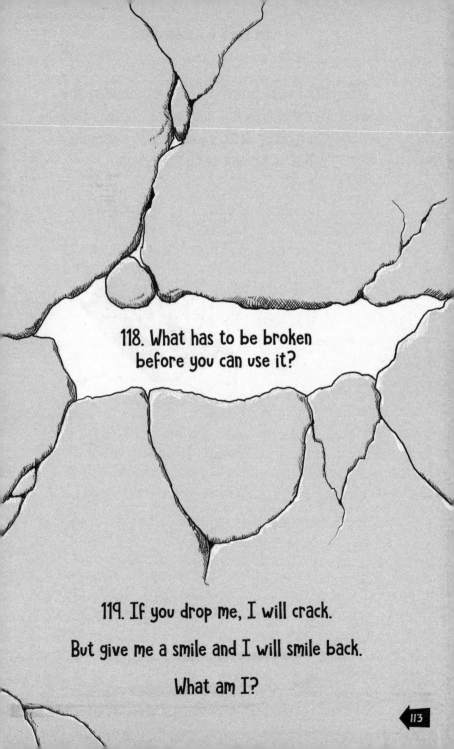

118. What has to be broken
before you can use it?

119. If you drop me, I will crack.

But give me a smile and I will smile back.

What am I?

120. Misha was boasting that on holiday she went swimming every day in a beautiful lake where the water was a lovely 20° Fahrenheit. What is wrong with this claim?

121. What has six faces
and 21 spots?

122. Here is a road, watch out for the cars. How do you spell that without any 'r's?

123. What do a comb, a zip and a crocodile all have in common?

124. An electric train leaves London at 9 a.m. It heads north to Scotland. The wind is blowing from east to west. In which direction does the steam from the train travel?

125. How do you turn the Roman numeral IX into six with one mark of your pen?

IX

126. I give you life, you draw me in. I'm ever present but never seen. What am I?

127. I always follow my brother, though he's very different to me. You see him, but you can't see me. You hear me, but you can't hear him. What am I?

128. What do you find at the end of the rainbow?

129. Once you have it, you want to share it. Once you share it, you don't have it. What is it?

130. Mrs Khan has organized a summer picnic for her class. She asks everyone to bring an item for the picnic. She writes a list of names and what each student must bring:

APPLES - Ahmed

CHEESE - Caitlin

EGGS - Ethan

LEMONADE - Lily

ROLLS - Roberto

STRAWBERRIES - Shannon

She has accidentally left one child off the list: Theo. But he has worked out what he needs to bring. What could it be?

131. Professor Cosmo, a well-known astronomer, was doing some research in his laboratory one night when he started to receive a code on his computer. The code read:

Far from being worried, the professor was extremely excited by this otherworldly message. What did the message say?

132. Which word is the odd one out?

BALLOON

TATTOO

RABBIT

TOFFEE

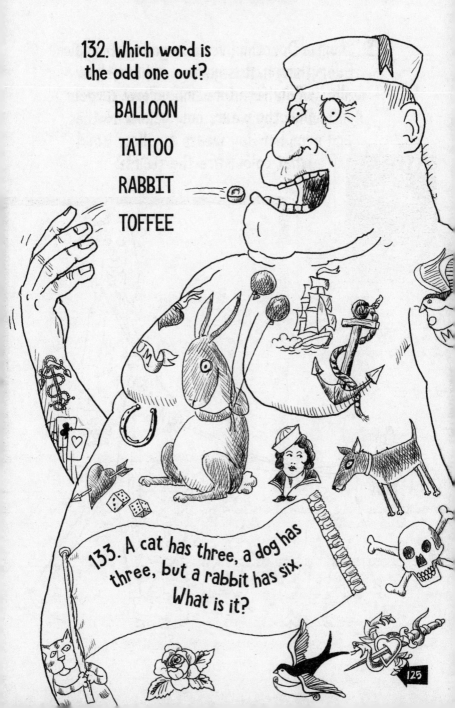

133. A cat has three, a dog has three, but a rabbit has six. What is it?

125

134. Auntie Dorothy lives in a yellow bungalow.
Everything in it is yellow: it has yellow
walls, yellow furniture and yellow carpets.
Auntie Dorothy wears only yellow clothes,
and even her dog wears a yellow bow!
What colour are the stairs?

135. How many peas are there in a pod?

136. What time of day is spelled the same forwards and backwards?

137. Pedro is from Brazil. He has one brother and one sister, who both also live in Brazil and have children. But Pedro's nieces and nephews don't call him 'Uncle Pedro'.
Why is this?

138. A woman enters a café and asks for a glass of water. The café's owner claps his hands and shouts loudly in her face. She thanks him and leaves. Why did this happen?

139. When asked about his pet cats, Paul replies that all but two are black, all but two are tabby and all but two are ginger. How many cats does he have?

140. You come home to find your mother's sister's only brother-in-law washing your car. Who is he?

141. Poppy the cat can jump higher than 150 cm, but when she tries to jump through a window that is 130 cm high, she fails. Why is this?

142. A cowgirl rides into town on Friday, stays for three days and leaves on Friday. How did she do it?

143. You are trapped in a labyrinth and come to a fork that leads to two paths. Two huge beasts stand guard. One of them says:

"One of our paths will lead you to freedom. The other path will lead to your doom. One of us is a truth-teller, the other tells only lies."

You do not know which beast is which. You can ask one question to only one of the beasts. What do you ask?

144. What is full of holes but can still hold water?

145. What goes around a garden but doesn't move?

146. What two things can you never eat for dinner?

147. Ling and her mum have just returned from the supermarket. Ling's mum is carrying three heavy bags of shopping, and she makes Ling carry four bags. You might think this sounds unfair, but Ling doesn't mind at all. Why is this?

148. How can you smell if you don't have a nose?

149. One hot day, Mrs Shah popped out to buy ice pops as a treat for her class of 30 children. She bought five lemon-flavoured, five strawberry, ten cola and fifteen orange. Unfortunately, three of them melted on the way back. What did she do?

150. At Pippa's birthday party, there are six children, including Pippa. They are all the same age. Pippa's two parents are also the same age as each other. Their ages all contain the same single number, and their combined age is 112. How old are the children and the parents?

151. In 4 years, Lila will be twice as old as she was 4 years ago. In 2 years, she will be twice as old as she was 5 years ago. How old is she?

152. Miles comes from a big family. His mum, Deborah, has parents called Fred and Felicity. Miles has three aunts (Anne, Amelia and Abigail) and two uncles (Boris and Bob). He has four siblings (Mia, Matthew, Miranda and Maddie). What are Fred and Felicity's daughters' names?

153. Two princes are in love with the same princess. They ride their horses to her to ask for her hand in marriage. To help her decide who to marry, she declares:

"You must race your horses across the city. I will marry the prince whose horse passes the city gates LAST by sundown."

The princes set off. They both ride as slowly as possible in the hope that they will be the last to arrive at the city gates to win the princess's hand in marriage. But they go SO slowly that the princes realize they will never reach the city gates by sundown.

Then, they remember the princess's words, "I will marry the prince whose horse passes the city gates last ..." This gives them an idea. Just minutes later, one of the princes has won her hand in marriage. What was their idea?

154. Danny and his wife have a car that seats up to five people. Danny drives Susie to work every day. He drops three of his children at school, then he drops his eldest daughter at college. How does he fit everyone in the car?

155. Emma is going on holiday and has packed five pairs of socks, two pairs of gloves and two pairs of trousers. How many individual items of clothing does she have?

157. Cheng is arranging his toy trucks in a row. What is the smallest number of trucks he has if:

A green truck is placed to the left of a blue truck.

A blue truck is placed to the left of a green truck.

Two trucks are placed to the right of a green truck.

158. There are 7 months with 31 days, and 4 months with 30 days. Which of the months has 28 days?

159. Isabel and Imogen are sitting in the same room, at the same table, with their eyes open and the lights on. Why can't they see each other?

160. Jamie and Julia both eat half a pizza. They eat nothing else, yet one of them eats more than the other. How is this possible?

161. Miss Green is walking around the classroom checking her students' answers to a sum. The sum is 150 – 144. She leans over Billy's desk, sees the number 9 and marks his work with a big cross. Billy is sure that his answer is correct. How does he prove that he's right?

162. A thief has been locked in a prison cell. There is nothing in the cell except a dirt floor and a rusty old spoon. On the wall is an unbarred window, but it is too high up to reach, and there is no furniture to stand on. The thief decides the only way to escape would be to dig his way out with the spoon. He starts digging, but soon realizes it will take far too long and he doesn't even know if the tunnel will lead anywhere. Then he comes up with a new plan and several days later he escapes. How did he do it?

Answers

1. None of them – it's a coconut tree.

2. Water – cows don't drink milk.

3. Baby elephants

4. A cloud

5. A stamp

6. In the sea

7. A map

8. The match

9. Mohammed

10. It will take each chef the same amount of time to chop an onion, so ten chefs will take 5 seconds to chop ten onions.

11. A glove

12. She asked him if he was asleep, and he replied "yes" so was clearly lying.

13. An icicle

14. They come from a melted snowman.

15. He slept at night not during the day!

16. Five

17. We know that Ben brought the cookies.

    We know that someone brought the cupcakes AND dressed as a ghost.

Therefore, Ben dressed either as a zombie or a skeleton.

If someone brought cupcakes AND dressed as a ghost, that rules out Callie, who either brought pasta OR dressed as a skeleton. Since the pasta is the only food item left, Callie must have brought it. This means that she dressed as a zombie and, therefore, Ben dressed as a skeleton.

So, Aman brought the cupcakes and dressed as a ghost.

18. She fell off the bottom step.

19. A kite

20. He mixes the yellow and blue paints together to make green.

21. It was driven over when the lake was frozen.

22. The wind

23. The third child – they live in a round house, so there are no corners.

24. Eight (and two thumbs)

25. Your right hand

26. Second

27. Breath

28. The chef – he said he was making breakfast, but that's not true as Mr Simpson was killed in the afternoon.

29. Footsteps

30. The other end of the lead wasn't attached to anything.

31. A person riding a horse.

32. Roller skates

33. The door of her van.

34. They both weigh a kilo.

35. Roosters are male birds and don't lay eggs.

36. Sunday – today is Saturday.

37. No, he throws an ordinary ball straight up in the air.

38. Romeo and Juliet were goldfish. The cat knocked the goldfish bowl off the table, smashing the glass and eating the fish.

39. Mrs McDonald is 36 years old.

40. He is your dad.

41. The third person is a newborn baby.

42. When you're a mouse.

43. It was daytime.

44. A vampire bat

45. A candle

46. Sand

47. He is still alive.

48. Playing table tennis with Sofia.

49. She juices the oranges and serves 23 equal portions of the juice.

50. Pears – he only sells fruits that grow on trees (the others either grow on vines or bushes).

51. An eraser

52. Because it will be midnight and dark.

53. One of the farm workers was bald.

54. Ten – they are the same trees.

55. None

56. Just one big pile

57. 21 – each number is the sum of the two numbers before it: 1 + 2 = 3, 2 + 3 = 5, 3 + 5 = 8, 5 + 8 = 13, 8 + 13 = 21

58. Six

59. 0–0 – the score of any game before it starts.

60. There are ten including Sophie.

61. Your name

62. Stella

63. Turn off the tap

64. Six – there's only one brother.

65. Because it only has 28 (or 29) days.

66. Zero

67. Once – the next time you'd be taking 10 from 90.

68. Turn over the 2-minute hourglass and place the egg in the boiling water. When it runs out, immediately turn over the 3-minute hourglass. When this runs out, turn over the 2-minute hourglass again, and take the egg out when it has run out.

69. Your sister

70. You took four oranges, so you have four.

71. A tree

72. Whatever your name is – remember, YOU are the bus driver.

73. Door 2: remember, the electricity isn't working so the door won't hurt you!

74. Eight – he eats two a day.

75. Paper

76. He is not tall enough to reach the button for the 20th floor on the way up. He can only reach the button to the 5th floor.

77. She wrote 'your exact weight' on the piece of paper.

78. She chooses the South End hair salon. As they are the only hairdressers in town, they must cut each other's hair.

79. The criminal chose to die of old age.

80. Naomi and Ana go first, as their combined weight is 100 kg. When they reach the other side, Naomi gets off and Ana rows back to David. Ana then gets off and David gets on the boat, rows to the other side and gets off. Naomi gets on the boat and rows back on her own to get Ana. Together, Naomi and Ana row back to join David on the other side.

81. Melon. Jenni only likes food that needs the outer layer removed before you eat it.

82. The parrot is deaf.

83. Wait until night-time, then take the first door.

84. Draw a shorter line next to the first line and it will appear longer.

85. 1, 2 and 3

86. Toby is a horse, Rosa is his rider.

87. The food items are all available in colours other than red. The jam (for example) could be apricot jam, the apples could be yellow or green, and the peppers could be green or orange.

88. Stop imagining!

89. There are only three people – a grandfather, his son and his grandson.

90. Five

91. On the child's head

92. Temperature

93. 15 – it doubles in size every day, so the day before it was full, it was half full.

94. "What is today's date?"

95. 1. Olivia 2. Ramesh 3. Petra 4. Harry

96. Three. Two frogs decided to jump, but this doesn't mean they actually jumped off the lily pad.

97. Time

98. An echo

99. A hole

100. Music

101. It's a pencil with an eraser on the end.

102. Anika

103. The letter 't'

104. He is a pilot in the cabin of an aeroplane.

105. Two horses in a field. (Flies refer to the insects on their bodies.)

106. A ghost

107. A snake

108. The letter 'a'

109. The children should pick envelope 1.

    They know that only one envelope has a true statement written on it; the other two are false. The statements written on envelopes 2 and 3 say the complete opposite of one another, meaning that one of them must be true. If envelope 2 was the true statement that would mean that envelope 1 was also true – and there can only be one true statement out of the three. So the true statement must be envelope 3. This means that envelope 2 and envelope 3 do not contain the key, so the children should pick envelope 1, which, despite what the envelope says, does contain the key.

110. The word 'wholesome'

111. A dandelion

112. When they are flipped vertically they still look the same.

113. The bus driver is off-duty so isn't driving his bus – he is walking.

114. Chilli

115. A mountain

116. The word 'wrong'

117. They are all types of bed.

118. An egg

119. A mirror

120. 20° Fahrenheit is below freezing, so she wouldn't have been able to swim as the lake would have been frozen solid.

121. A dice

122. The word 'that' has no 'r's.

123. They all have teeth.

124. There is no steam – it's an electric train.

125. Draw an 'S' in front of the numeral so it becomes the word SIX.

126. Air

127. Thunder (lightning is the brother)

128. The letter 'w'

129. A secret

130. Anything beginning with 't' (e.g. tomatoes). Each item starts with the first letter of the child's name.

131. 'I COME IN PEACE'. Read the letters from the top to the bottom of each column, starting in the top left corner.

132. Rabbit. The other three words all have two double letters in a row.

133. Letters in its name

134. There are no stairs – it's a bungalow.

135. There's just one 'p' in pod.

136. Noon

137. They are Brazilian so they speak Portuguese. (They would call him 'Tio Pedro'.)

138. The woman had hiccups, so he gave her a shock to help get rid of them.

139. Three – one is black, one is tabby and one is ginger.

140. Your father

141. The window is closed.

142. Her horse is called Friday.

143. Ask either beast "If I were to ask the other beast 'Which path leads to freedom?' what would they say?"

Scenario 1: If the question is directed at the truth-teller, they would tell you the truth that the liar would point to the path that leads to doom.

Scenario 2: If the question is directed at the liar, he would tell a lie and point to the path which leads to doom.

So, either way, you know for sure which path leads to doom.

144. A sponge

145. A fence

146. Breakfast and lunch

147. Ling's shopping bags are empty.

148. By not taking a shower.

149. She didn't need to do anything – she had bought 35 ice pops, so there were still enough ice pops to go around.

150. 4 and 44 years old

151. 12 years old

152. Anne, Amelia, Abigail and Deborah

153. To switch horses. Each prince, let's say Prince A and Prince B, is riding a horse: let's call them Horse A and Horse B. If Horse A is slower, Prince A wins the princess's hand in marriage. If Horse B is slower, Prince B wins. Neither prince wants to reach the city gates FIRST, as they will not win. So, when they switch horses, Prince A is now riding Prince B's horse (Horse B) and Prince B is riding Prince A's horse (Horse A). Now they both want the horse they're riding (which is the other prince's horse) to reach the city gates FIRST, because the slower horse will win.

154. Susie is the name of the car.

155. 16 (ten socks, four gloves and two pairs of trousers)

156. You can't dig half a hole. (There's no such thing – a hole is a hole.)

157. Four trucks

158. They all have at least 28 days.

159. They're sitting with their backs to each other.

160. They ate the halves of two different pizzas. One pizza is bigger than the other.

161. He turns the book around to show the number '6' (it was upside down).

162. He digs enough dirt to create a mound to stand on, reach the window and make his escape.

ALSO AVAILABLE:

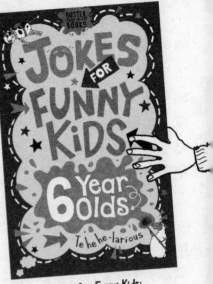

Jokes for Funny Kids:
6 Year Olds
ISBN: 978-1-78055-626-0

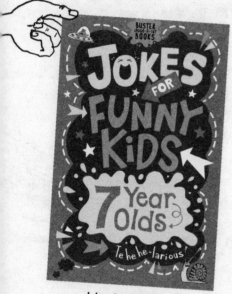

Jokes for Funny Kids:
7 Year Olds
ISBN: 978-1-78055-624-6

Jokes for Funny Kids:
8 Year Olds
ISBN: 978-1-78055-625-3